W9-BXE-196

Diabetes

BY MICHELLE LEVINE

amicus
high interest

Amicus High Interest is an imprint of Amicus
P.O. Box 1329, Mankato, MN 56002
www.amicuspublishing.us

Library of Congress Cataloging-in-Publication Data
Levine, Michelle, author.
Diabetes / by Michelle Levine.
    pages cm — (Living with . . .)
Summary: "Describes what it is like to live with diabetes, what
its symptoms are, and how it is treated"— Provided by publisher.
Includes bibliographical references and index.
ISBN 978-1-60753-480-8 (library binding) —
ISBN 978-1-60753-693-2 (ebook)
1. Diabetes. I. Title.
RC660.L45 2013
616.4'62—dc23
                                        2013034064

Editors   Kristina Ericksen and Rebecca Glaser
Series Designer   Kathleen Petelinsek
Designer Heather Dreisbach
Photo Researcher: Kurtis Kinneman

Photo Credits: Fertnig/iStockphoto, cover; Rob Lewine/Tetra
Images/Corbis, 5; Diego Cervo/Shutterstock, 6; Zurijeta/
Shutterstock, 9; Science Photo Library/SuperStock , 10; Jaimie
Duplass/Shutterstock, 13; BSIP SA/Alamy, 14; Benedicte
Desrus/Alamy, 17; Blend Images/Alamy, 18; BSIP SA/Alamy,
21; Thomas Imo/Alamy, 22; Science Photo Library/Alamy, 24;
Gallo Images/Alamy, 27; Okea | Dreamstime.com, 29

Printed in the United States of America at Corporate Graphics
in North Mankato, Minnesota.

10 9 8 7 6 5 4 3 2 1

Table of Contents

What Is Diabetes? 4

What Causes Diabetes? 8

Types of Diabetes **15**

Treating Diabetes 19

Living with Diabetes **24**

Glossary 30

Read More **31**

Websites 31

Index 32

What Is Diabetes?

Everyone is in class. So are you. But you don't feel well. Your mouth is dry. You're thirsty. You feel shaky and tired. You raise your hand. You go to the nurse. She has your medicine. It's for **diabetes**.

Being really tired can
be one sign of diabetes.

Playing takes lots of energy. Your body needs fuel to keep going.

 How many people have diabetes?

Diabetes is an illness. It affects how the body uses sugar. Sugar is like fuel. It gives the body energy. Your muscles need energy. Your brain needs it, too.

Too much sugar is unhealthy for anyone. But it is dangerous for people with diabetes. Their bodies do not use it properly.

 In the United States, more than 25 million people do. Most are adults. About 215,000 are children and teens.

What Causes Diabetes?

Crunch! Apples are juicy and sweet. Yum! But what happens after you eat one? The apple has sugar in it. You use it for fuel. It enters your blood. Your body makes **insulin**. Insulin is very important. It helps sugar leave your blood. Then it can go to other parts of your body.

An apple is a healthy snack for everyone.

This is a close-up view of the pancreas. It is a part of the body that makes insulin.

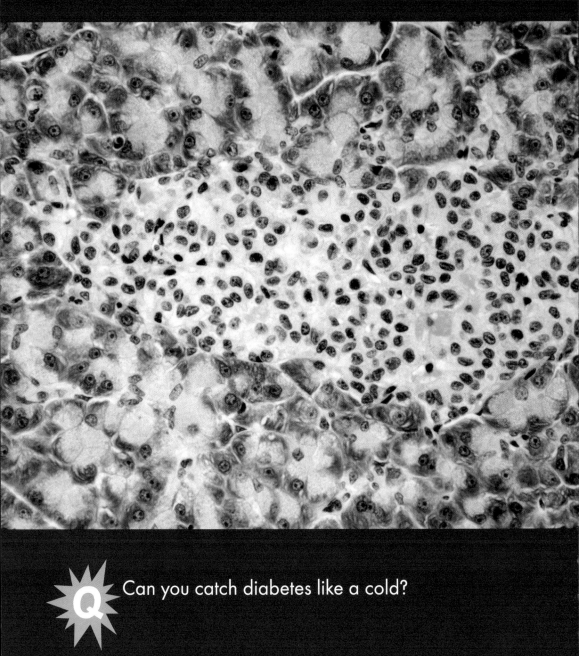

 Can you catch diabetes like a cold?

People with diabetes have problems with insulin. They may have too little. Or their bodies don't make any. Other people's bodies do not use insulin right. But in all cases, people with diabetes get high **blood sugar**. When they eat, sugar goes to the blood. But it gets stuck. High blood sugar is dangerous. It can make a person very sick.

 No. It is not **contagious**.

High blood sugar causes many **symptoms**. It makes people tired and shaky. It also causes thirst and hunger. It can cause weight loss, too. Tingly feet and blurry eyes are also symptoms. So is going to the bathroom a lot. These are warnings. You may have diabetes.

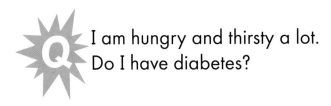
I am hungry and thirsty a lot. Do I have diabetes?

It is normal to drink lots
of water. But people with
diabetes are always thirsty.

 There are many reasons for hunger and thirst.
You may be growing. You may be exercising.
Or you may have diabetes. See a doctor if you
are worried.

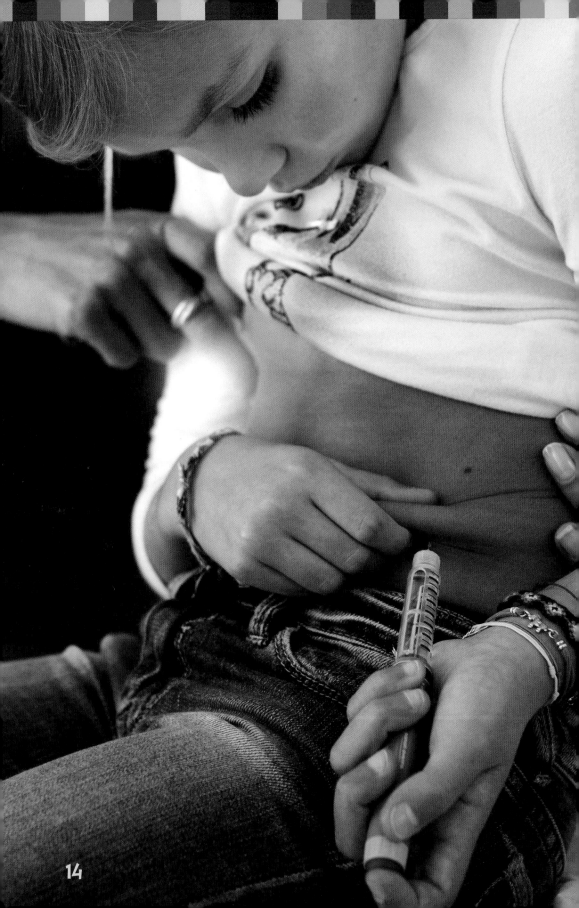

Types of Diabetes

There are two kinds of diabetes. One is called type 1. Younger people get type 1. Some adults get it too. People with type 1 do not make insulin. Or they make very little. Their bodies cannot use sugars safely. It gets trapped in their blood. Type 1 is not very common.

This girl gives herself medicine. She knows when she needs it.

15

The other kind of diabetes is type 2.
Most people with diabetes have this type.
They are usually over forty years old.
But younger adults can also get it. So
can children. People with type 2 make
insulin. But their bodies do not use it
the right way.

 What causes type 2?

People can get type 2 diabetes at any age.

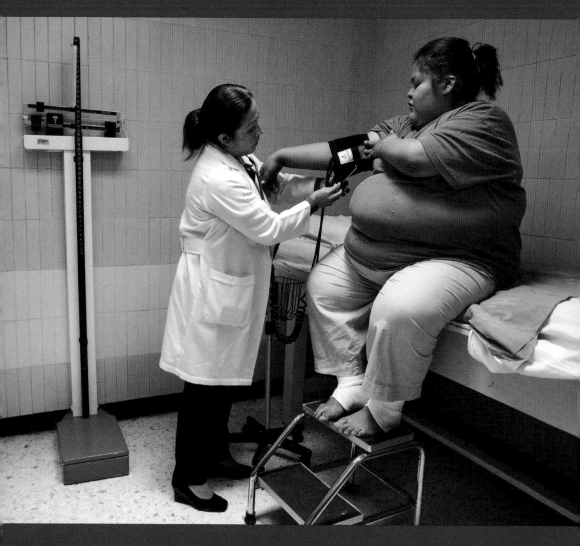

 One big cause is weight. Weighing too much can lead to the illness. But not everyone with type 2 is overweight.

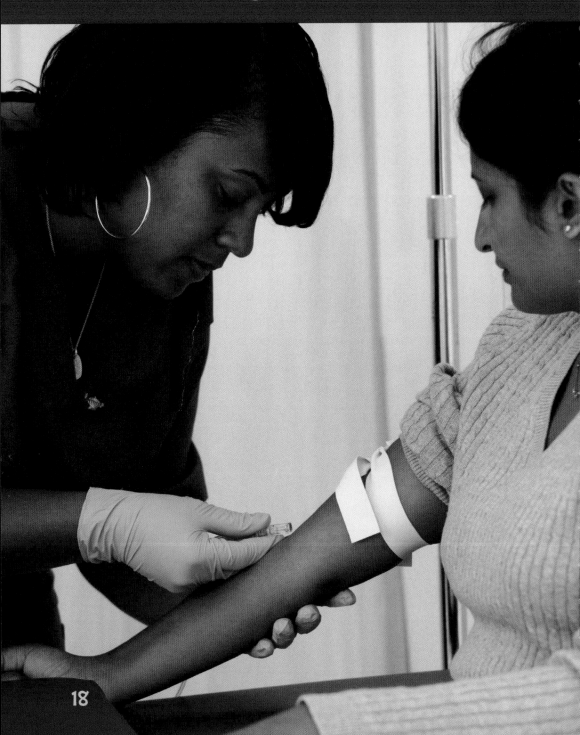

This woman is having a blood test. She might have diabetes.

Treating Diabetes

Diabetes can occur suddenly. You may be healthy for years. Then something changes. You feel sick. You have the symptoms of high blood sugar. You go to a doctor, who orders blood tests. The tests measure your blood sugar. They show whether or not you have diabetes.

There is no cure for the illness. But medicine helps. People with type 1 take medicine. They take insulin. People **inject** it as a shot. The shot lowers their blood sugar. It keeps them healthy. Many people with type 1 take insulin before meals. It helps a person use the sugar from food.

 Is there any other way to get insulin?

People with diabetes need lots of supplies for their treatment.

A Some people use a pump. This machine attaches to the body. It pumps in insulin.

This boy chooses his snack carefully. He will stay away from sugary foods.

 What are sugary foods?

People with type 2 diabetes have different ways to treat it. Some people with type 2 take insulin. Others take medicines. Many don't take anything at all. They are careful about what they eat. All people with diabetes avoid eating too many sugary foods. Being overweight can make type 2 worse. Some people work on losing weight.

Sweets are sugary. But so are starchy foods. **Starches** are in pastas, breads, and some vegetables. The body turns these foods into sugar.

Living with Diabetes

People with diabetes must test their blood sugar often. They use a **glucose meter**. It tests a tiny drop of blood. It tells them if they need an insulin shot. It also helps them plan what to eat. Some people test their blood many times a day. Others test it a few times a week.

The glucose meter looks like a pen. It takes a drop of blood from a person's finger.

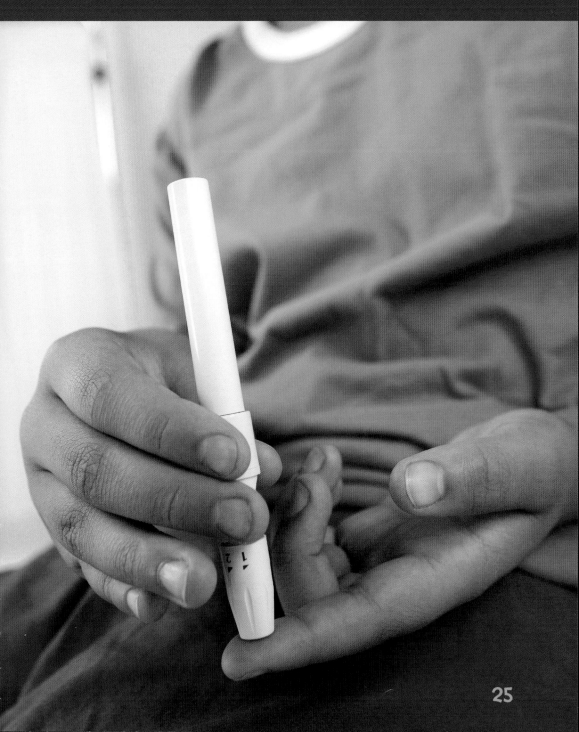

Sometimes a person takes too much insulin. Or they don't eat enough. They feel sweaty and dizzy. They feel weak and confused. Their breath smells fruity too. So they test their blood sugar. The machine says it is too low. Low blood sugar is dangerous. They need to eat something sugary fast. Juice is a good choice. Its sugars get to the blood quickly.

Sometimes, people with diabetes need something sweet.

Do you have friends with diabetes? Exercise with them. That will help lower their blood sugar. Offer them low-sugar foods. Vegetables and whole grains are great snacks. Remind them to check their blood sugar. And get help if they feel sick. Then everyone can have fun!

You can help your friends make healthy choices.

Glossary

blood sugar The amount of sugar in a person's blood. Both high and low blood sugar can be dangerous.

contagious A sickness that spreads from person to person.

diabetes An illness that affects how a person's body uses sugar.

glucose meter A small device used at home to test blood sugar.

inject To give medicine with a shot.

insulin Something the body makes that allows it to use sugars as fuel.

starch A part of some foods that is turned into sugar inside the body.

symptom Something caused by an illness or health problem.

Read More

Bryan, Jenny. *I Have Diabetes.* New York: Gareth Stevens, 2011.

Loughrey, Anita. *Explaining Diabetes.* Mankato, Minn.: Smart Apple Media, 2010.

McAuliffe, Bill. *Diabetes.* Mankato, Minn.: Creative Education, 2012.

Websites

Diabetes Information for Children and Teens
www.ndep.nih.gov/teens/

For Parents & Kids: American Diabetes Association
www.diabetes.org/living-with-diabetes/parents-and-kids/

Kids Health: Diabetes Center
kidshealth.org/kid/centers/diabetes_center.html

Every effort has been made to ensure that these websites are appropriate for children. However, because of the nature of the Internet, it is impossible to guarantee that these sites will remain active indefinitely or that their contents will not be altered.

Index

blood sugar 11, 12, 19, 20, 24, 27, 28
blood tests 19
causes 8, 11, 12, 16, 17
doctors 13, 19
energy 7
insulin 8, 11, 15, 16, 20, 21, 23, 24, 27
sugar 7, 8, 11, 15, 20, 22, 23, 27, 28
symptoms
eyesight 12
hunger 12, 13
thirst 4, 12, 13
tired 4, 12
weight loss 12
treatment
food 20, 22, 23, 27, 28
medicine 20, 23
type 1 diabetes 15, 20
type 2 diabetes 16, 17, 23

About the Author

Michelle Levine has written and edited many nonfiction books for children. She loves learning about new things—like diabetes—and sharing what she's learned with her readers. She lives in St. Paul, Minnesota.